special occasions
in lace

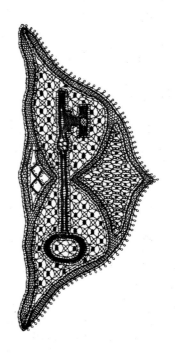

special occasions

in lace

Edited by Bridget M. Cook

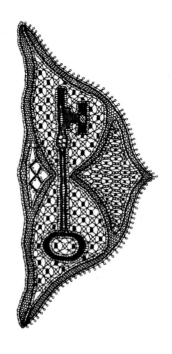

B T Batsford Ltd, London

Publisher's Acknowledgement
The publishers would like to acknowledge the contribution of Bridget M. Cook to this book, in both its overall compilation and co-ordination, and the production of the prickings and working diagrams.

Liz Tibbetts contributed greatly to the concept, and the publishers would like to acknowledge her involvement.

First published 1997

© B.T. Batsford Ltd 1997

ISBN 0 7134 7791 1

Designed by Peter Higgins
Printed in Hong Kong

A CIP record for this title is available from the British Library

Published by
B T Batsford
583 Fulham Road
London SW6 5BY

Contents

List of contributors and their patterns   6
The international colour-coding system   7
Helpful hints on presentation   7

The patterns
Red Heart Valentine by Elaine Merritt   10
Poinsettia Mat by Hilary Butler   12
Lucky Clover Coaster by Bridget M. Cook   14
Engagement Ring Collar by Bridget M. Cook   16
Love Bunny Duo by Bridget M. Cook   18
Oval Heart Frame by Bridget M. Cook   19
Super Star Window Hanging or Mat by Bridget M. Cook   20
Key to the Door Handkerchief Corner by Liz Tibbetts   22
Home Sweet Home by Liz Tibbetts   24
Through the Keyhole by Liz Tibbetts   25
New Driver's Key Ring by Liz Tibbetts   26
Mortar Board by Liz Tibbetts   27
Graduate's Scroll by Liz Tibbetts   28
Swaddling Baby by Liz Tibbetts   29
Confirmation by Liz Tibbetts   30
New-born by Liz Tibbetts   31
Alphabet by Liz Tibbetts   32
Thanksgiving Card by Gerlinde Simon   34
Mother's Day Card by Jean Horne   36
Birthday Balloons Coaster by M. Alison Dews   38
Spectacular Presentation Buttons by Meriel A Mattle   40
Birthday Tie Panel by Lesley J. Thomas   41
Dove of Peace by Marie-Christine Gosse   42
Christmas Tree Basket by Tordis Berendt   44
Gold or Silver Wedding Heart Handkerchief by Pat Milne   46

Sources of information   48

List of contributors

Elaine Merritt:	Red Heart Valentine
Hilary Butler:	Poinsettia Mat
Bridget M. Cook:	Lucky Clover Coaster
	Engagement Ring Collar
	Love Bunny Duo
	Super Star Window Hanging or Mat
	Oval Heart Frame
Liz Tibbetts:	Key to the Door
	Handkerchief Corner
	Home Sweet Home
	Through the Keyhole
	New Driver's Key Ring
	Mortar Board
	Graduate's Scroll
	Swaddling Baby
	Confirmation
	New-born
	Alphabet
Gerlinde Simon:	Thanksgiving Card
Meriel A. Mattle:	Spectacular Presentation Buttons
Jean Horne:	Mother's Day Card
M. Alison Dews:	Birthday Balloons Coaster
Lesley J. Thomas:	Birthday Tie Panel
Marie-Christine Gosse:	Dove of Peace
Tordis Berendt:	Christmas Tree Basket
Pat Milne:	Gold or Silver Wedding Heart Handkerchief

The international colour-coding system

The drawings for all the projects in the Batsford Lace Library have been prepared using the colour-coding system that has been established as the world standard:

Red: Clothstitch and twist (cross, twist, cross, twist) Wholestitch and twist

Purple: Clothstitch (cross, twist, cross) Wholestitch

Green: Halfstitch (cross, twist)

Yellow: The movement of an individual thread. This colour is frequently used to indicate the movement of a gimp thread.

Blue: A two-pair plait

Black: A coarse pair is a mixed threaded pair with one thread thicker than its partner, which is the same thread as used in the rest of the lace. This pair outlines the lace.

Helpful hints for presentation

Mounting lace onto fabric

Select a cloth of a similar weight and feel as the work when mounting the lace.

To attach the lace choose the thread used to create the work or one slightly thicker (and therefore stronger), especially if it is very fine. Choose a needle compatible with the work. A very fine oversewing stitch is the simplest when attaching lace to an existing hem.

Be warned that ready-made handkerchiefs and traycloths may not be truly square or rectangular. The lace should be made to fit the longest side and it can be then gently eased onto any slightly shorter sides. Care should be taken when mounting onto fabric without a hem that the pinholes lie correctly on the weave of the material. For straight edges it is sensible to draw a thread. Pin and tack carefully and attach into every hole of the footside using mock hem stitch, four-sided stitch or a triangular stitch.

On completion of the sewing cut carefully close to the edge. For extra strength and for particularly fine work do not cut too closely. Either roll carefully and whip back the raw edge or, alternatively, make a second row of four-sided stitch. Use a backing of coloured paper for very fine lace and for attaching to net. This will keep the lace in its correct shape and will help to identify the holes for sewing. Pin and tack the lace right-side-down on the paper and then tack the net on top. Oversew the lace to the net, including any motifs inside the border. Then remove the paper and cut the net close to the edge.

Mounting in frames or purpose-bought mounts

Use a small scrape of clear-drying general-purpose PVA adhesive dabbed onto the back of a denser part of the work. Secure the work to the chosen backing material and assemble the frame. Glass, perspex and thick clear PVC film (acetate) are all suitable to protect the work.

Antique frames can often be found and one should always be on the lookout for these. They can be very satisfying and particularly suitable for lace work. Modern purpose-made craft mounts can be in the form of trinket boxes, jewellery, frames, key rings and powder compacts. They all have different methods of holding the craft work in place but all should come with clear instructions.

For paperweights, wedge with a spacer of thick dark card, under the lace and its backing, if needed to keep the work from slipping, and finish with a disc of sticky-backed suede vinyl.

Special mounts can be expensive but most designs can be mounted just as effectively on ready-cut cards. Many shapes and sizes are available including bookmarks, gift tags and shapes of sufficient size for large pictures. The best will have a ready-cut aperture behind which the design is fixed with a double fold of card so that the fixing of the work is obscured. For a professional finish protect the work with a thin clear PVC sheet cut slightly larger than the aperture and glued to the back of it.

Different backings of card or fabric can create different results and add an ingredient to the gift or occasion. Silk or velvet is luxurious, but beware of deep pile for fine work as the lace can sometimes move with the pile if handled.

Other ideas for mounting lace

For a permanent and durable finish iron on clear protective coverings as used for covering pressed flowers, in satin matt finish. This seals directly onto most flat surfaces and is ideal for finishing wood mounts such as clock faces, boxes or small wood blocks for making brooches or pendants.

Lace made with thicker thread does not necessarily need to be mounted or covered. Mats and bookmarks can be stiffened with a weak solution of starch or ironed with spray starch. In order to avoid squashing the work place the right side down onto a soft pad and press lightly. A special preparation, such as the stiffener used to make roller blinds, can be used to stick and seal lace to a backing fabric or to stiffen the piece from a light finish to one that is rock-hard. In this way small pieces of work can be stiffened to make jewellery. In order to avoid clogging or opaqueness use thinned and apply several coats until the desired stiffness is obtained. Stiffeners are also required for any 3-D work or lace that is to be hung. This can include a wall or window hanging as it also protects the lace from dust and dirt.

Many of the mounts and fixings can be found in craft suppliers', model shops, florists' and stationers'. Seek out something different, and be inventive in order to create that special lace gift for family or friends.

Red Heart Valentine

Elaine Merritt   USA

Bobbins: 23 pairs
Gimps: 1 pair
Thread: DMC 50 Broder Machine or
         equivalent Crochet cotton for the
         gimp pair

Six of the pairs can be in a contrasting colour if
desired. These are the passive pairs at foot and
headside and three passives in the cat-stitch
section. The last coloured pair is the worker for
the hearts and this pair is carried from heart to
heart with the gimp.

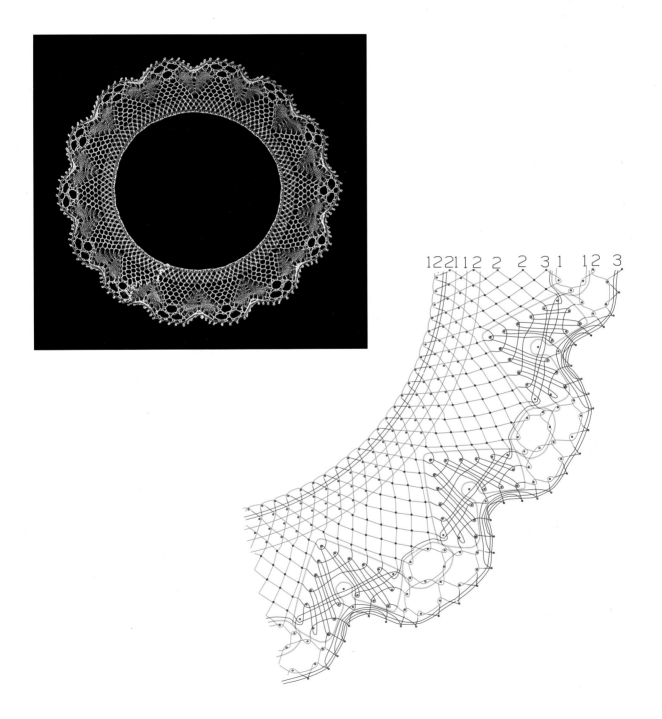

Poinsettia Mat

Hilary Butler   UK

Bobbins: 46 pairs
Gimps: 4 pairs plus one single gimp
Thread: 30 Madeira cotton
         Cotton perlé no. 5 for the gimps

This can be made in colour.

Lucky Clover Coaster

Bridget M. Cook   UK

This coaster is made in two sections. Make the outside first.

Outside:
Bobbins: 14 pairs
Thread: 50 Egyptian Cotton

Complete this outside ring. Then sew in as needed for the inner section.

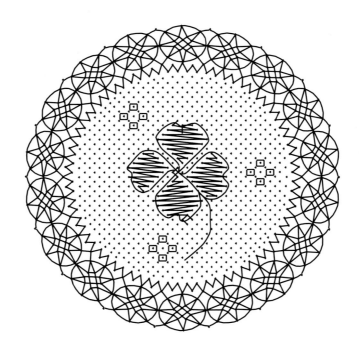

Inner section
Bobbins: 44 pairs
Gimps: 2 pairs
Thread: 50 Egyptian Cotton
         Cotton perlé no. 12 for the gimps

On completion sew out all pairs into the inner
edge of ring.

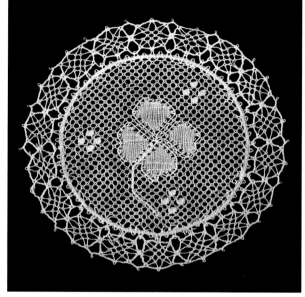

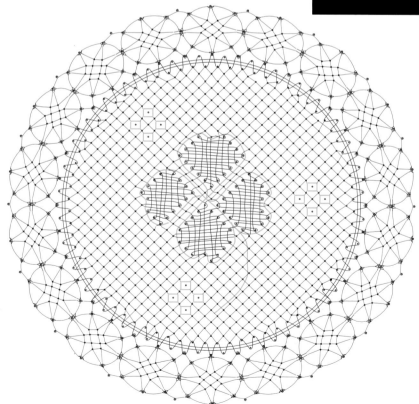

15

Engagement Ring Collar

Bridget M. Cook   UK

Bobbins: 31 pairs
Gimps: 2 pairs
Thread: 50 Egyptian Cotton
         Cotton perlé no. 8 for the gimps

Two sections make up a complete collar.
Reverse the pattern for the second section.

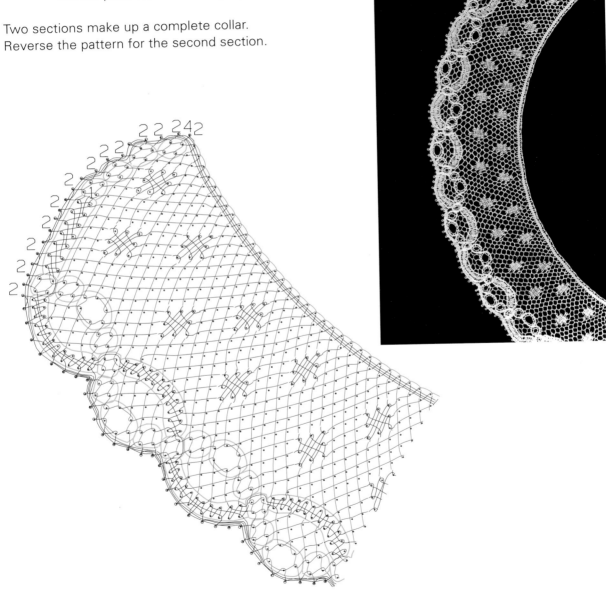

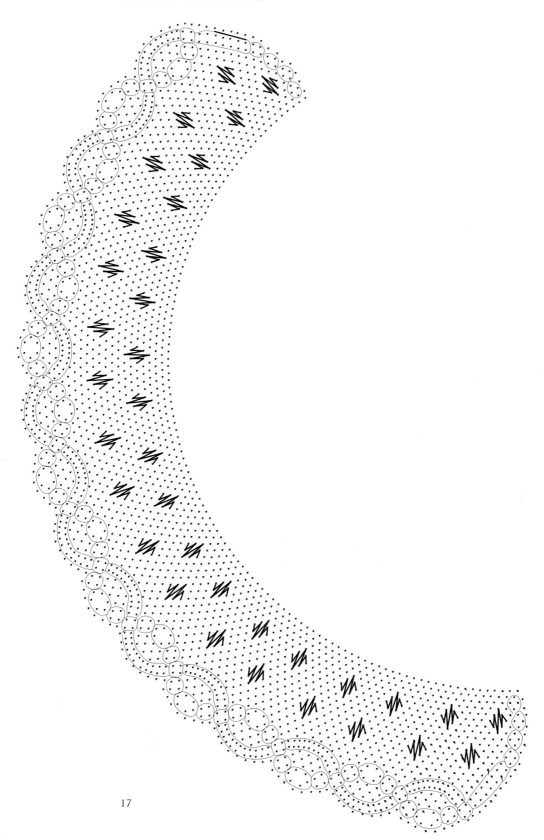

Love Bunny Duo

Bridget M. Cook   UK

Bobbins: 69 pairs
Gimps: Several, as required
Thread: 80 Egyptian Cotton
         Cotton perlé no. 12 for the gimps

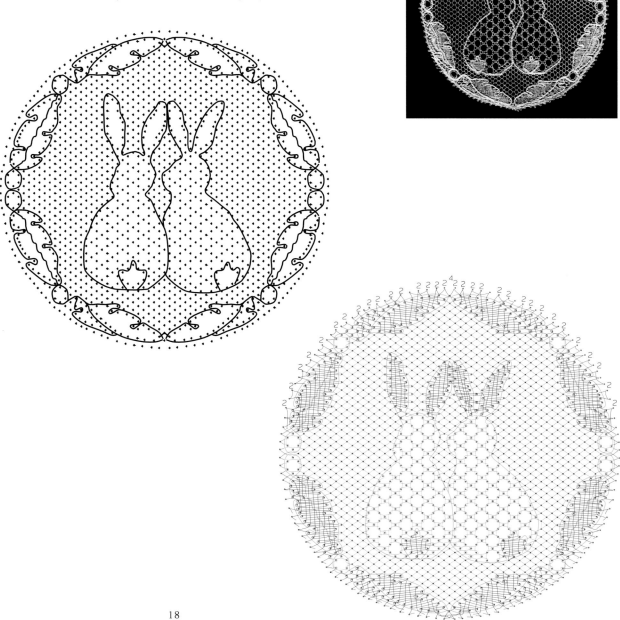

Oval Heart Frame

Bridget M. Cook   UK

Bobbins: 13 pairs
          1 gimp pair
Thread: 50 Egyptian Cotton
          Cotton perlé no. 8

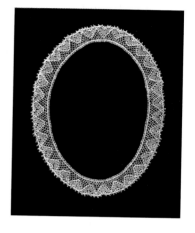

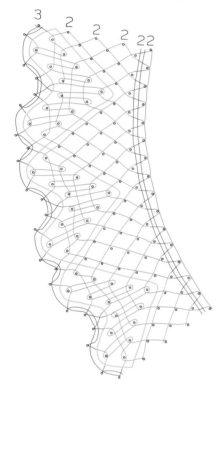

Super Star Window Hanging or Mat

Bridget M. Cook UK

Bobbins: 11 pairs
Thread: 80 DMC Cordonnet Special

Seven points make the complete star.
Only three are given in the pricking. Photocopy
the pricking and make up a complete star.

Start in the centre and work up one side of
the first point and down the second side.
Then work up the second point and so
continue. On completion sew off, tie and cut
all pairs except the centre pair. The centre pair
works around the centre sewing in each
pinhole before also being tied and cut off.

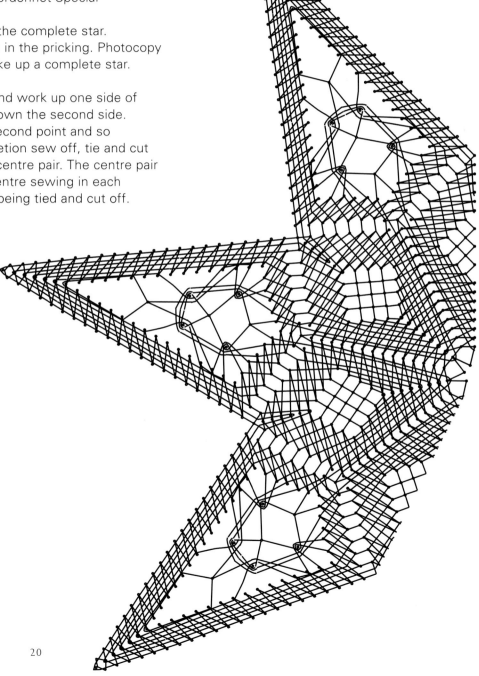

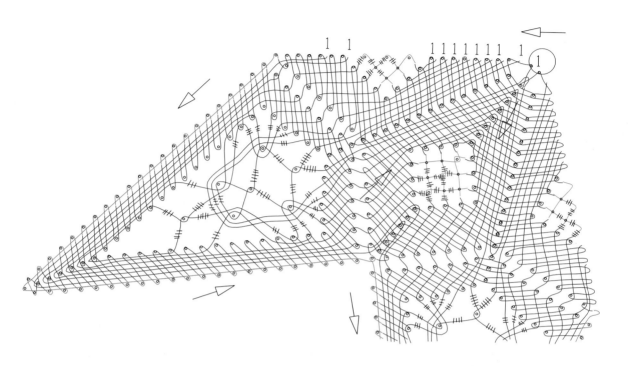

Key to the Door Handkerchief

Liz Tibbetts   UK

Thread: Brok Cotton 120/2
            Coarse thread - Coats traditional
            soft cotton

The diagram has been separated into two
sections for clarity.

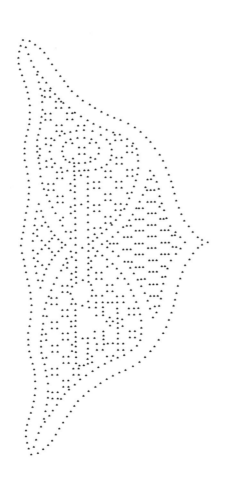

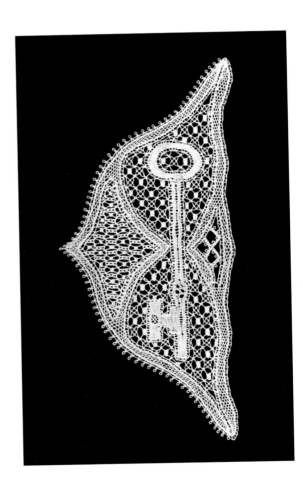

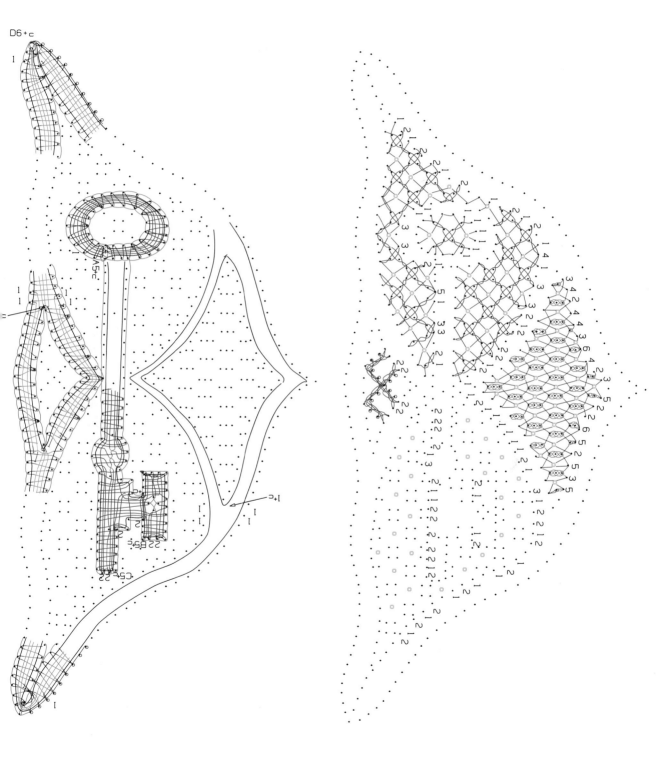

Home Sweet Home

Liz Tibbetts   UK

Thread: Brok Cotton 120/2
         Coarse thread - Coats traditional soft cotton

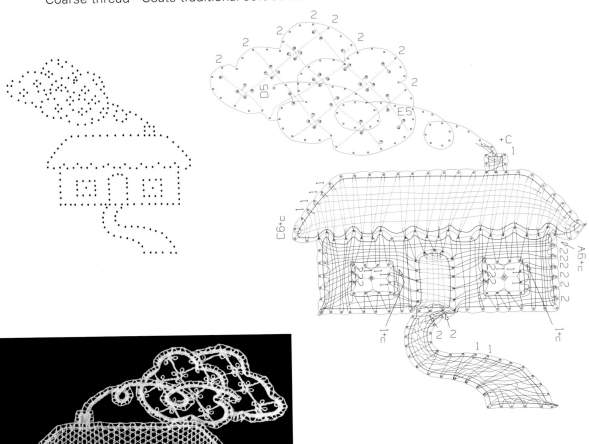

Through the Keyhole

Liz Tibbetts   UK

Thread: Brok Cotton 120/2
         Coarse thread - Coats traditional soft cotton

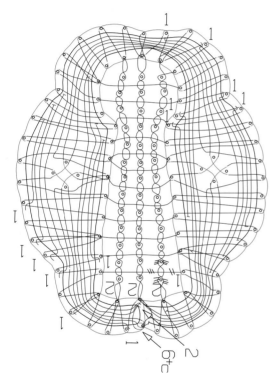

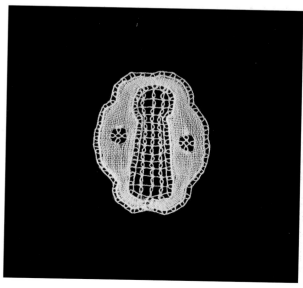

New Driver's Key Ring

Liz Tibbetts   UK

Thread: Brok Cotton 120/2
Coarse thread - Coats
traditional soft cotton

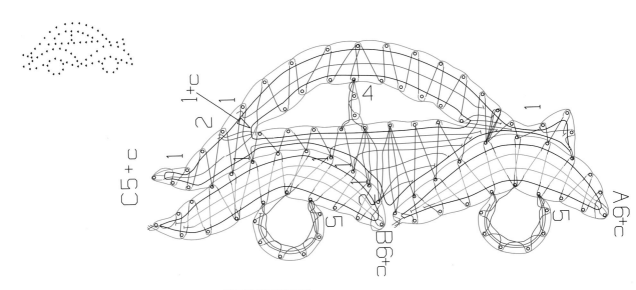

Mortar Board

Liz Tibbetts   UK

Thread: Brok Cotton 120/2
         Coarse thread - Coats
         traditional soft cotton

For clarity the diagram has been divided
into two sections.

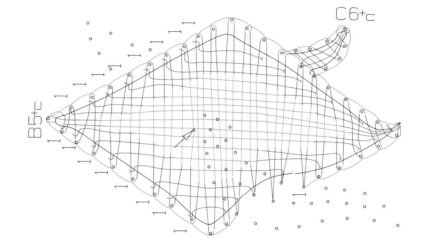

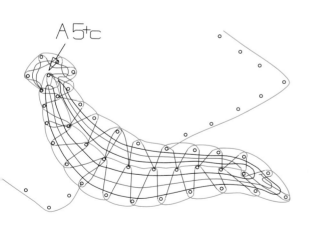

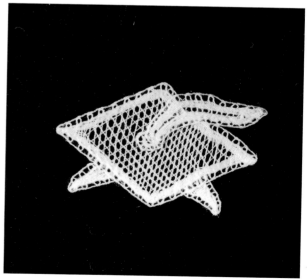

Graduate's Scroll

Liz Tibbetts   UK

Thread: Brok Cotton 120/2
Coarse thread - Coats traditional
soft cotton

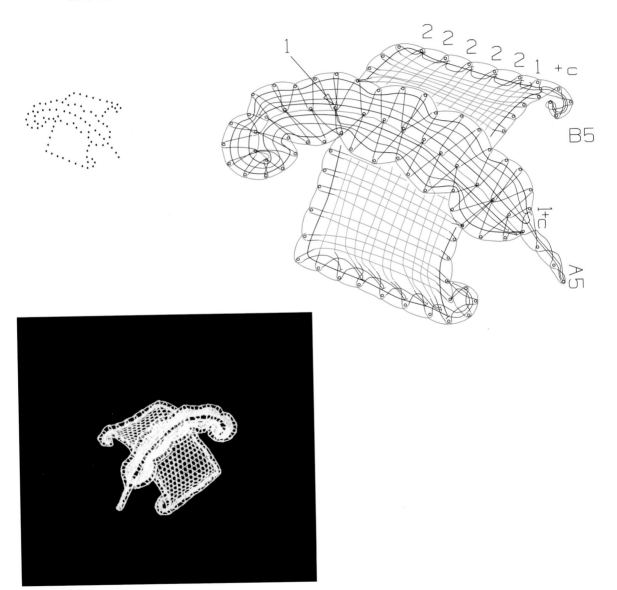

Swaddling Baby

Liz Tibbetts   UK

Thread: Brok Cotton 120/2
           Coarse thread - Coats traditional
           soft cotton

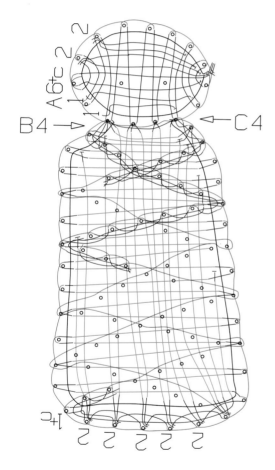

Confirmation

Liz Tibbetts   UK

Thread: Brok Cotton 120/2
          Coarse thread - Coats traditional
          soft cotton

For clarity the diagram has been divided into
two sections.

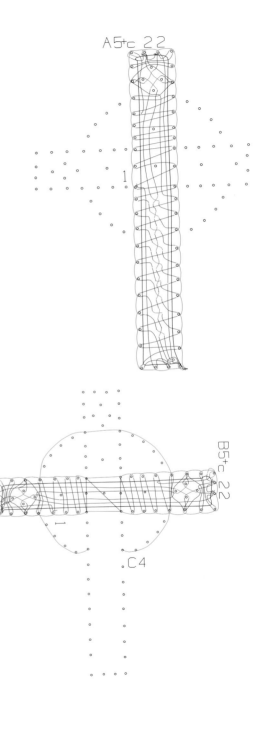

New-born

Liz Tibbetts   UK

Thread: Brok Cotton 120/2
         Coarse thread - Coats traditional
         soft cotton

For clarity the diagram has been divided into
two sections.

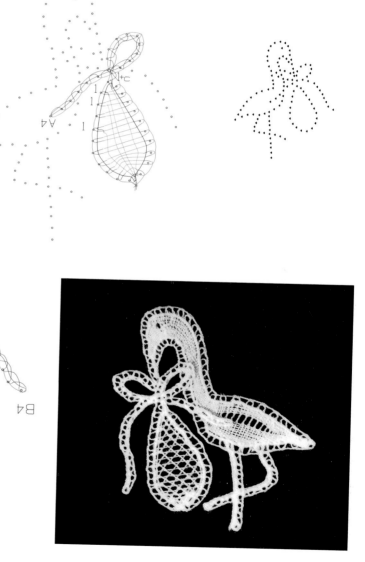

Alphabet

Liz Tibbetts UK

These motifs can be used for personalizing any design

Thread: Brok Cotton 120/2
        Coarse thread - Coats traditional
        soft cotton

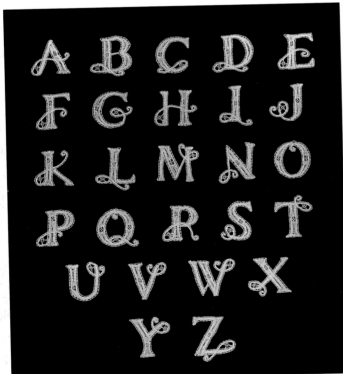

Thanksgiving Card

Gerlinde Simon   Germany

A presentation basket with cake and wine

Thread: 100/3 Silk, Mez 80 or Linen 80/2

Order of working

The frame
Bobbins: 5 pairs

The flowers
Bobbins: 3 pairs

The basket
The cake
Bobbins: 3 pairs

Use large pins for this section

Bottle

Start at the bottom. Sew off and tie but always leave the pairs in case they can be carried and used in another section. The number of twists vary according to the shape required.

The completed lace should be stiffened.

Mother's Day Card – "Joy for Mother's Day"

Jean Horne   South Africa

Thread: 80 DMC Special dentelle or similar

Start with the left-hand figure working the pairs
from the head through the arm to the bottom. Pairs
may need to be added and removed at the sides of
the dresses. On completion of the first figure make
the mother from head to toe and then the last child
on the right.

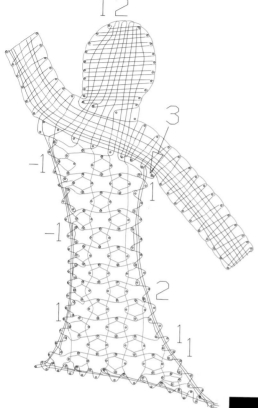

Birthday Balloons Coaster

M. Alison Dews   UK

Bobbins: 6 pairs in white for the trail
               42 pairs in white plus
               2 pairs coloured for the workers
               (use a colour suitable for the occasion)
Thread: 40 Madeira Cotton
               30 Broder Machine for the gimp

This coaster is made in two sections. Make the outside first.

Outside

Bobbins: 6 pairs
Thread: 40 Madeira Cotton

Complete this outside ring. Then sew in where needed for the inner section.

Inner section

Bobbins: 42 pairs plus two coloured pairs for the
worker pairs of the balloons.
Gimps: 2 pairs
Thread: 40 Madeira Cotton
30 Broder Machine for the gimps

On completion sew out all pairs into the inner
edge of the ring.

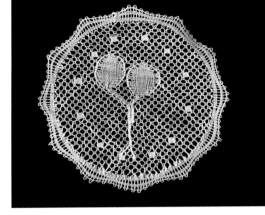

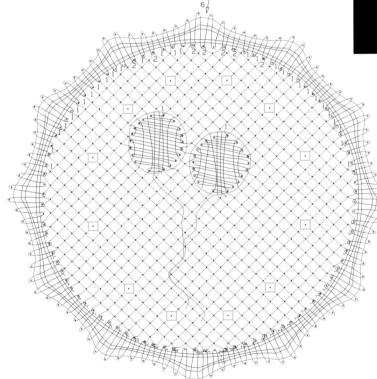

Spectacular Presentation Buttons

Meriel A. Mattle   Switzerland

Thread: a coloured thread to suit the size and
shape of the button mould.

Cover the button mould with silk. Sew on the
completed motif with invisible thread.

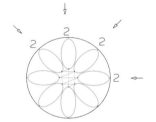

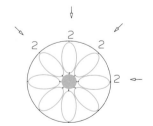

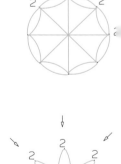

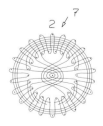

Birthday Tie Panel

Lesley J. Thomas   UK

Bobbins: 18 pairs
Thread: 100/3 Gutermann silk

Work 44 cms of pattern to create the panel,
which is then appliqued to a suitable plain tie.
End of lace can be tucked into finishing seam.

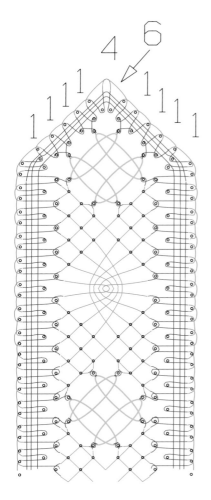

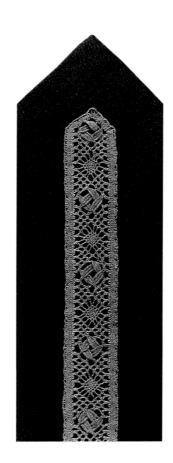

Dove of Peace – mobile for a new baby

Marie-Christine Gosse   France

Thread: 50/2 Madeira Cotton

Brass wire is used as a gimp along the outer
edge; this stiffens it and makes it self-supporting.
Work braids in numbered sequence.

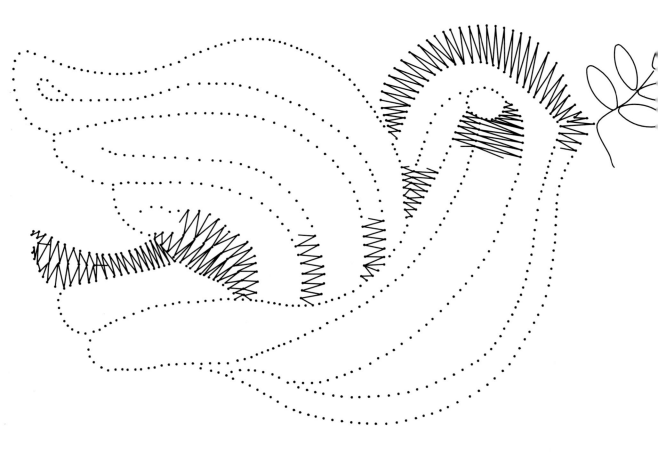

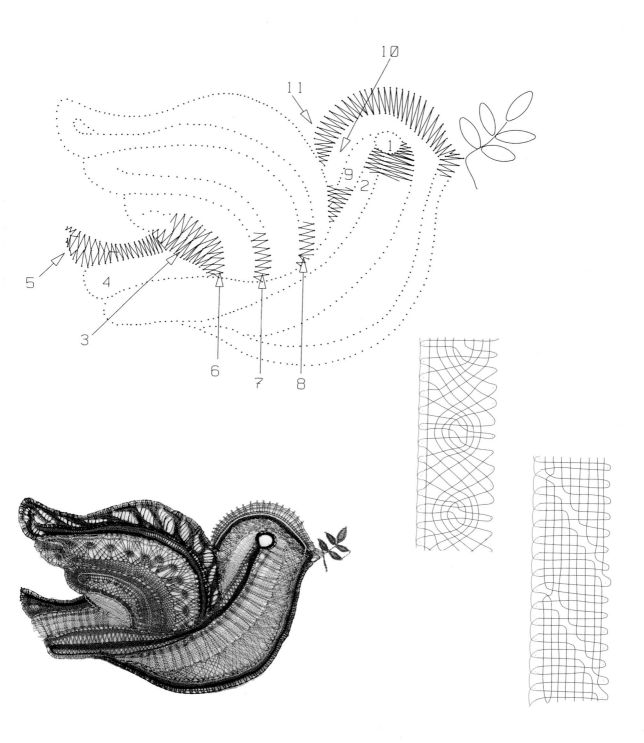

Christmas Tree Basket
Christmas Tree Decoration

Tordis Berendt   Denmark

Bobbins: 8 pairs
Thread: 80 DMC Cordonnet Special

Make the basket and join the lower sections to
form the basket. Add the handle. Finally curl
down the halfstitch sections.

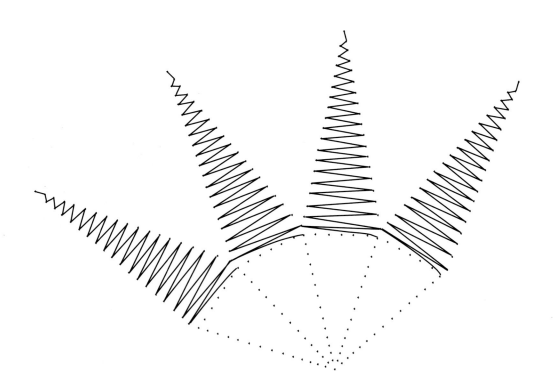

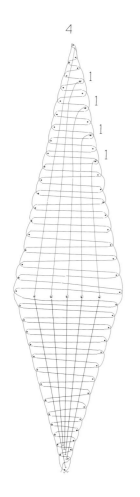

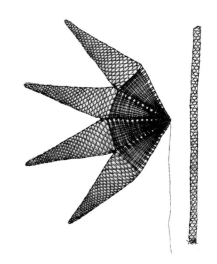

Gold or Silver Wedding Heart Handkerchief — a torchon heart

Pat Milne   Australia

Bobbins: 14 pairs
          1 gimp pair
Thread: 50 DMC Retors d'Alsace
          Silver or gold gimp thread
          (Twilley's goldfingering)

For the Dieppe ground, halfstitch, pin, halfstitch and twist.

For the headside use extra twists to ensure that it is firm.

2 2 2 2 2 211

Sources of information

UNITED KINGDOM

The Lace Guild
The Hollies
53 Audnam
Stourbridge
West Midlands DY8 4AE

OIDFA
Tamara Golding
'Nonsuch Too'
27 Ollands Road
Reepham
Norfolk
NR10 4EL

**The British College
of Lace**
21 Hillmorton Road
Rugby
Warwickshire CV22 5DF

International Old Lacers
Ann Keller
Cool Valley
Abingdon Park
Shankill
Dublin

The Lacemakers' Circle
20 Ulverscroft Road
Loughborough
Leicester
LE11 3PU

The Lace Society
Lynwood
Stratford Road
Oversley, Alcester
Warwickshire B49 6PG

Ring of Tatters
Miss B. Netherwood
269 Oregon Way
Chaddesden
Derby DE21 6UR

AUSTRALIA

Australian Lace Guild
National Committee
Box Hill
Victoria 3128

Australian Lace
Magazine
P.O. Box 609
Manly
NSW 2095

BELGIUM

OIDFA
Alice de Smedt
Welvaartstraat 149
B 9300 Aalst
Alg. Spaar-en-Lijfentekas

**Belgische
Kantorganisatie**
Irma Boone
Gentse Steenweg 296
B-9240 Zele

FRANCE

OIDFA
Suzanne Puech
3 Chemin de Parenty
F-69250 Neuville sur
Saône

GERMANY

OIDFA
Uta Ulrich
Papenbergweg 33
D-32756 Detmold

**Deutscher
Klöppelverband
e.V**
Schulstr. 38
D-52531
Übach Palenberg

Klöppelschule
Nordhalben
Klöppelschule 4
D-96365 Nordhalben

THE NETHERLANDS

OIDFA
Elly De Vries
Couwenhoven 52-07
NL-3703 ER Zeist

LOKK
Boterbloem 56
NL-7322 GX Apeldoorn

SWITZERLAND

**Fédération de
Dentellières**
Suisses
Evelyne Lütolf
Buhnstrasse 12
CH-8052 Zürich

USA

OIDFA
Elaine Merritt
5915 Kyburz Place
San José CA 95120

International Old Lacers
Editor
Julie Hendrick
2737 NE 98th
Seattle WA 98115

**Point Ground Tours &
Publications**
124 W. Irvington Place
Denver
Co 80223-1539

OIDFA

(International Bobbin
and Needle
Lace Organization)

President
Lydia Thiels-Mertens
Jagersberg 1
B-3294 Molenstede-
Diest
Belgium

Vice President
Alice De Smedt
Welvaartstraat 149
B 9300 Aalst
Belgium